T0051587

1	2	3	4	5	6	7	8	9	10
11	12	13	14	15	16	17	18	19	20
21	22	23	24	25	26	27	28	29	30
31	32	33	34	35	36	37	38	39	40
41	42	43	44	45	46	47	48	49	50
51	52	53	54	55	56	57	58	59	60
61	62	63	64	65	66	67	68	69	70
71	72	73	74	75	76	77	78	79	80
81	82	83	84	85	86	87	88	89	90
91	92	93	94	95	96	97	98	99	100
101	102	103	104	105	106	107	108	109	110
111	112	113	114	115	116	117	118	119	120
121	122	123	124	125	126	127	128	129	130
131	132	133	134	135	136	137	138	139	140
141	142	143	144	145	146	147	148	149	150
151	152	153	154	155	156	157	158	159	160
161	162	163	164	165	166	167	168	169	170
171	172	173	174	175	176	177	178	179	180
181	182	183	184	185	186	187	188	189	190
191	192	193	194	195	196	197	198	199	200
201	202	203	204	205	206	207	208	209	210
211	212	213	214	215	216	217	218	219	220
221	222	223	224	225	226	227	228	229	230
231	232	233	234	235	236	237	238	239	240
241	242	243	244	245	246	247	248	249	250

1. **Two**

2. **Hundred**

3. **and**

4. **Fifty**

5. **Things**

247. **an**

248. **Architect**

249. **Should**

250. **Know**

Michael Sorkin

Princeton Architectural Press, New York

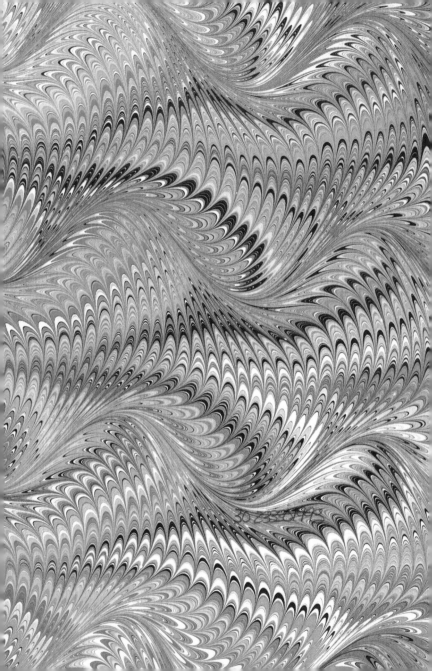

1. The feel of cool marble under bare feet

2. How to live in a small room with five strangers for six months

3. With the same strangers in a lifeboat for one week

4. The modulus of rupture

5. **The distance a shout carries in the city**

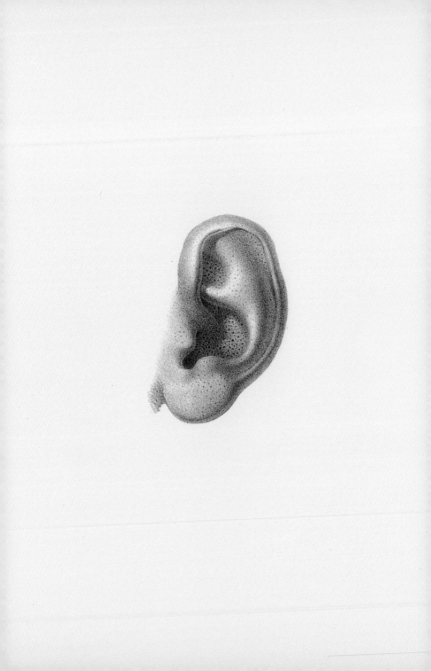

6. **The distance of a whisper**

7. Everything possible about Hatshepsut's temple (try not to see it as "modernist" *avant la lettre*)

8. The number of people with rent subsidies in New York City

9. In your town (include the rich)

10. **The flowering season for azaleas**

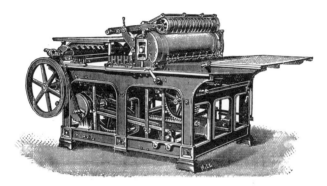

23.

24.

25.

How to

turn a corner

design a corner

sit in a corner

32. **The direction of prevailing winds**

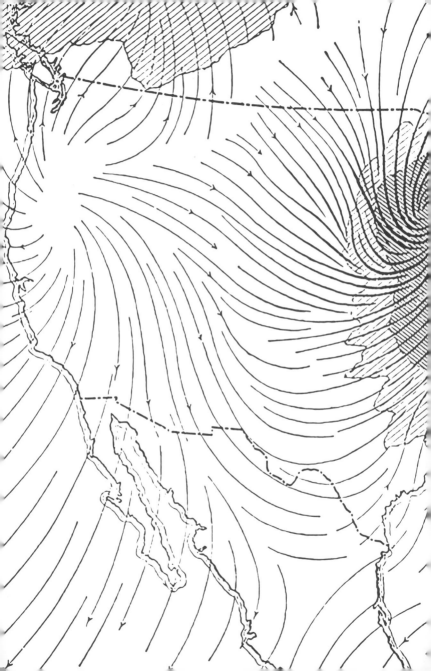

33. Hydrology is destiny

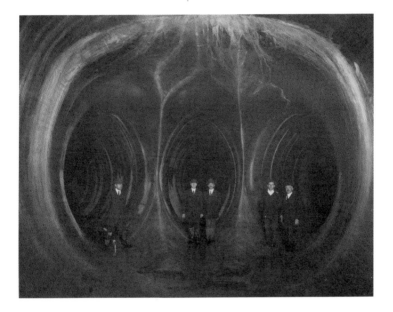

38. **The color wheel**

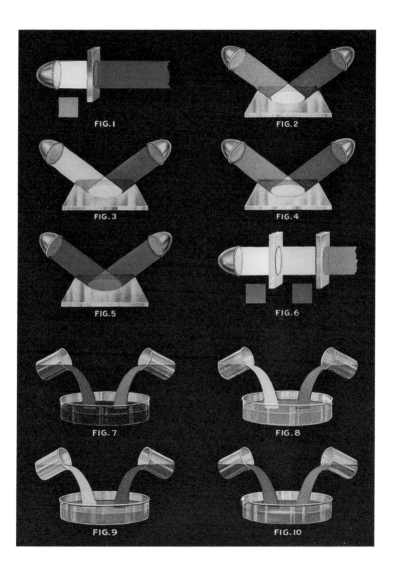

FIG.1

FIG.2

FIG.3

FIG.4

FIG.5

FIG.6

FIG.7

FIG.8

FIG.9

FIG.10

39. **What the client wants**

40. **What the client thinks it wants**

41. **What the client needs**

42. **What the client can afford**

43. **What the planet can afford**

47. **What the brick really wants**

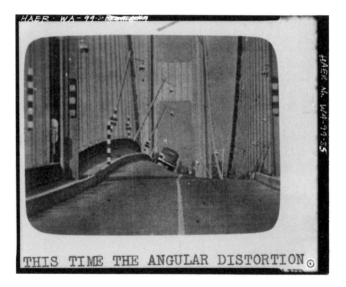

THIS TIME THE ANGULAR DISTORTION

58. Vitruvius

73. **The difference between a ghetto and a neighborhood**

74. How the pyramids were built

75. Why

76. The pleasures of the suburbs

77. The horrors

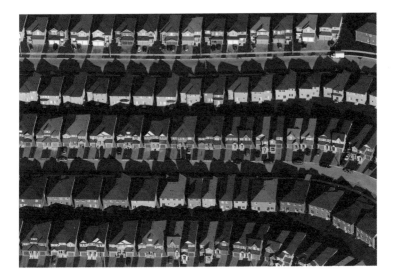

78. **The quality of light passing through ice**

95. Where materials come from

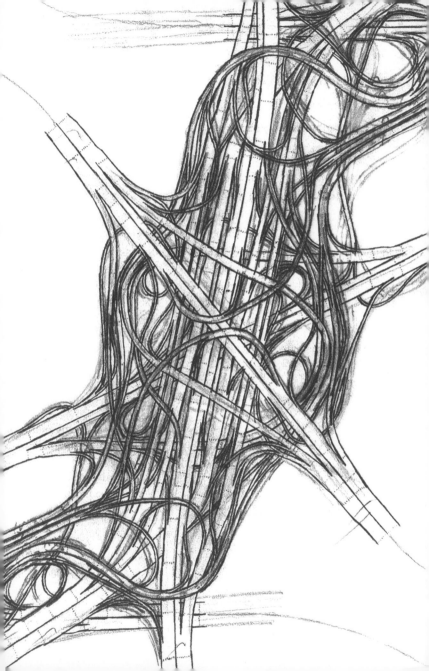

106. **Woodshop safety**

123. The Romantics, throughout the arts and philosophy

124. How to listen closely

125. That there is a big danger in working in a single medium. The logjam you don't even know you're stuck in will be broken by a shift in representation.

126. The exquisite corpse

127. **Scissors, stone, paper**

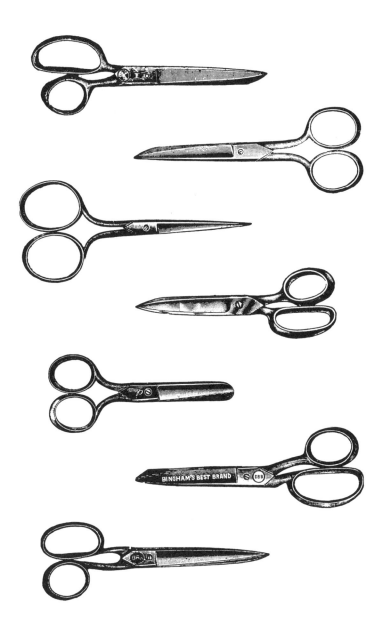

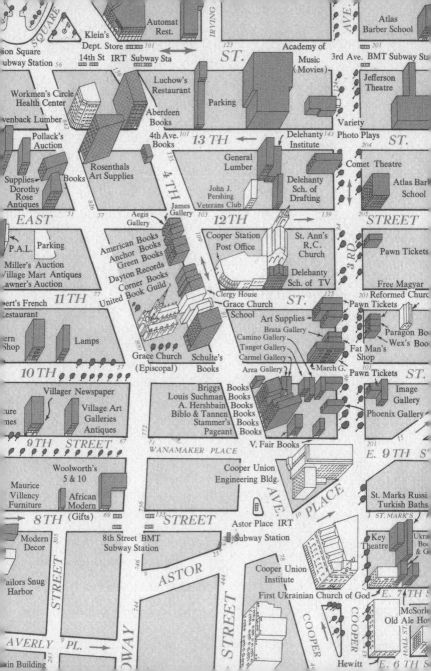

SQUARE

Klein's
Dept. Store

Automat
Rest.

IRVING

Atlas
Barber School

ion Square
ubway Station 56

14th St IRT Subway Sta

101

123

ST.

Academy of

201

3rd Ave. BMT Subway Sta

Music
(Movies)

Jefferson
Theatre

Workmen's Circle
Health Center

Luchow's
Restaurant

124

venback Lumber 842

Aberdeen
Books

Parking

Variety

Pollack's
Auction

4th Ave. 101
Books

13 TH

Delehanty 143
Institute

Photo Plays

ST.

204

Rosenthals
Art Supplies

135

General
Lumber

Delehanty
Sch. of
Drafting

Comet Theatre

Supplies

Dorothy
Rose
Antiques

Books

4 TH

John J.
Pershing
Veterans Club

Atlas Bar
School

51

826

57

James
Gallery

Aegis
Gallery

103

12TH

139

205

STREET

EAST

109

Cooper Station
Post Office

St. Ann's
R.C.
Church

84

P.A.L.

Parking

American Books
Anchor Books
Green Books
Dayton Records
Corner Books
United Book Guild

Pawn Tickets

Miller's Auction
illage Mart Antiques
awner's Auction

3 RD

Free Magyar

201 Reformed Church

ert's French
estaurant

11 TH

77

800

Clergy House
Grace Church
School

ST.

125

Pawn Tickets

Art Supplies

Brata Gallery
Camino Gallery
Tanger Gallery
Carmel Gallery

Paragon Bo
Wex's Boo

Fat Man's
Shop

ern
hop

Lamps

Grace Church
(Episcopal)

Schulte's
Books

Area Gallery

March G.

46

Pawn Tickets

ST.

10 TH

57

Image
Gallery

Villager Newspaper

Briggs Books
Louis Suchman Books
A. Hershbain Books
Biblo & Tannen Books
Stammer's Books
Pageant Books

Phoenix Gallery

cure
nes

Village Art
Galleries
Antiques

772

201

15

9TH

STREET

67

71

WANAMAKER PLACE

V. Fair Books

E. 9TH S

Woolworth's
5 & 10

Cooper Union
Engineering Bldg.

St. Marks Russi
Turkish Baths

Maurice
Villency
Furniture

African
Modern

756

AVE.

10 PLACE

3 ST. MARK'S

8 TH

(Gifts) 69

133 STREET

Astor Place IRT
Subway Station

Key
Theatre

Ukrai
Boo
& G

Modern
Decor

305

8th Street BMT
Subway Station

746

9

23

78

Cooper Union
Institute

E. 7TH S

ailors Snug
Harbor

744

ASTOR

First Ukrainian Church of God

COOPER

McSorle
Old Ale Ho

E. 7TH S

AVERLY

9 PL.

283

ain Building

WAY

STREET

444

COOPER

HALL ST

E. 6TH S

Hewitt

PLAN GENER.ᵃˡ DE VERSAILLES

Son Parc, Son Louvre, Ses Jardins,
Ses Fontaines, Ses Bosquets,
et sa Ville.

Par N. de Fer
Geographe de Monsig.ʳ
le Dauphin.

A PARIS
Chez le S.ʳ de Fer dans
l'Isle du Palais sur le
Quay de l'Orloge a la
Sphere Royale
Avec Privilege du Roy.
1700

Echelle de ....

Parc de S.ᵗ Cyr

S.ᵗ Cyr

Pointe de Galie

Grand Mail

Parc

Traverse du Canal

Chemin de Paris par S.ᵗ Germain

la Place des Suisses

Reserve

Place d'Armes

Ville

Neuve

la Paroisse

le Parc aux Cerfs

S.ᵗ de Conty

Chemin de Paris ou de la Reine

Avenue de Sceaux

Rue de Satory

Rue de Montreuil

Clagny

L'Etang

Resnoy
A. le Chât.
B. l'Oranger.
C. le Par.terre d'Eau.
D. Bassin de Neptune.
E. Font. du Dragon.
F. l'Arc de Triomphe.
G. les 3. Bosquets.
H. le Theatre d'Eau.
I. l'Etoille ou Mont. d'eau.
J. Salle des Fest.ins.
L. l'Enceladé.
M. les Bains à polon.
N. les 3. Bosquets.
O. le Marais ou Chesne vert.
P. Par.terre de la Piramide.
Q. la Salle du Bal.
R. le Labirinthe.
S. la Colonnade.
T. Salle des Antiques.
V. Bassin de Saturne.
X. Bassin de Flore.
Y. Bassin de Bacchus.
Z. Bassin de Ceres.
&. Bassin de Latone.
1. Pavillon de M.ʳ le Roy.
2. Pavil. de M.ʳ le Chancelier.
3. Pavil. de M.ʳ Chamillard.
4. Pavil. de M.ʳ de Chamineuf.
5. Pavil. de M.ʳ de Croissy.
6. le grand Commun.
7. le Potager.

181. **Dawn breaking after a bender**

189. Solid geometry

190. Strengths of materials
(if only intuitively)

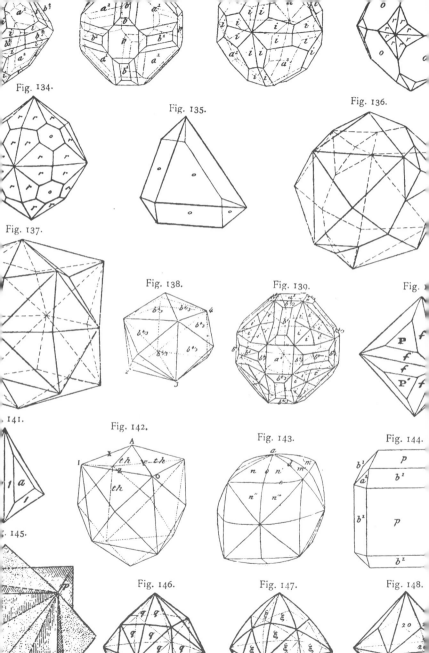

Fig. 134.

Fig. 135.

Fig. 136.

Fig. 137.

Fig. 138.

Fig. 139.

Fig. 140.

Fig. 141.

Fig. 142.

Fig. 143.

Fig. 144.

Fig. 145.

Fig. 146.

Fig. 147.

Fig. 148.

285. A. TONKIN — Baie d'Along
Parages des Merveilles

Elevated R. R. Curve at 110th Street, New York.

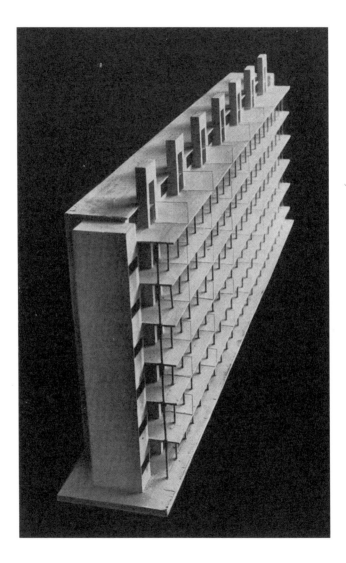

201. **Good model-making techniques in wood and cardboard**

202. **How to play a musical instrument**

203. **Which way the wind blows**

ETTEILLA.

♈

QUESTIONNANT.

♈

215. **How close is too close**

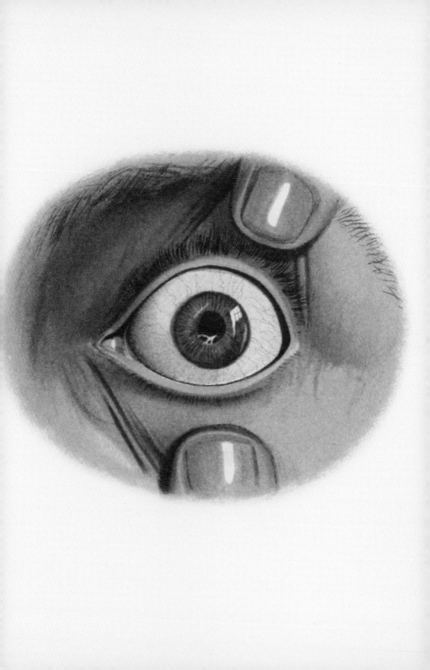

222. The diameter of the earth

223. The number of gallons of water used in a shower

224. The distance at which you can recognize faces

225. How and when to bribe public officials (for the greater good)

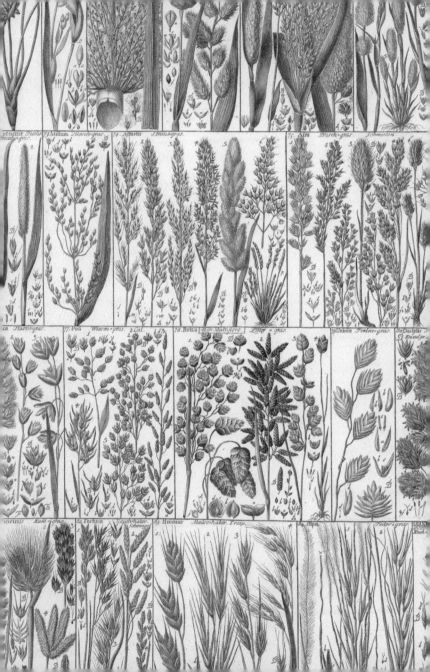

pecunit Parten
Knauligras.   77. Milium   Hirch-gras.   74. Agrostis   J Fill-gras.   75. Aira   Burch-gras.   Schmielen

ca Haar-gras.   77. Poa   Wiesen-gras.   2. Cal.   73   78. Briza   Glas Multifloro   Zitter-gras.   79 Uniola   Perlen-gras.   80 Dactyl
G. Knaulgr.

iorum   Kam-gras   82. Festuca   Gauch-haber   89. Bromus   Mauch-haber   Trespe   90. Stipa   Feder-gras.   URN
Schwing   Rauh-

234. **Rachel Carson**

235. **Freud**

242. **Your neighbors**

247. **The depths of desire**

A. W. Winterschmidt, sculps. excud.

248. **The heights of folly**

Michael Sorkin (1948–2020) was
a unique figure in the field of architecture.
His lucid and passionate diagnoses
of the rights and wrongs of the city excited
readers within and beyond the profession.
Fearless, acerbic, and never without wit,
he skewered self-serving power structures
and railed against inept design. His critical
skills were matched by his architectural
acumen, which was evidenced in countless
drawings, site plans, and models of
positive, wildly imaginative alternatives
to business-as-usual architecture.
His premature departure leaves us with
a voluminous archive of profoundly
influential words and designs, but without
the irrepressibly energetic, funny, generous,
and kind man who unleashed them—
the brilliant polymath and proponent
of an equitable, sustainable urban life.

Traditional Italian marbled paper
(detail). From New York Public
Library Picture Collection.

*Newsboys Climbing Iron
Grillwork Door, Havana,* 1933,
photograph by Walker Evans.
© Walker Evans Archive,
The Metropolitan Museum
of Art.

Human ear.
Tabulae Anatomicae
(New York: Macmillan,
1839), 212.

Azalea Pontica (detail).
From Rare Book Division,
Digital Collections, New York
Public Library.

Benson & Rixon Company building,
1938, photograph by Hedrich
Blessing Photographers. From
Irma and Paul Milstein Division
of United States History, Local
History and Genealogy, New York
Public Library.

Laying bricks in construction of
manhole at migrant camp at Sinton,
Texas, photograph by Lee Russell.
From Photography Collection,
Miriam and Ira D. Wallach Division
of Art, Prints and Photographs,
Digital Collections, New York Public
Library.

Printing press,
source unknown.

Hammurabi (detail). From Print
Collection, Miriam and Ira D.
Wallach Division of Art, Prints
and Photographs, Digital
Collections, New York Public
Library.

Eddying storm moving eastward
across the United States, 1888
(detail). Alex Frye, *The Child and
Nature: Or, Geography Teaching
with Sand Modelling* (Boston:
Ginn, 1888), 172.

Yonkers pressure tunnel.
Contract 54. November 21, 1913.
From General Collection,
Science, Industry and Business
Library, Digital Collections,
New York Public Library.

A 14th Street tree, clipping.
From Irma and Paul Milstein
Division of United States History,
Local History and Genealogy,
New York Public Library.

Mixing color. Guy Stanton
Ford, *Compton's Pictured
Encyclopedia and Fact-
Index*, vol. 3. (Chicago:
F.E. Compton, 1922), 454.

Workers trimming great
green wall on ladder, 1962.
From Bettman Collection /
Getty Images

Film still,
source unknown.

Hindi alphabet.
Published by Indian Book
Depot, New Delhi.

Roman Colosseum, date and
photographer unknown (detail).
From New York Public Library
Picture Collection.

Tacoma Narrows Bridge, spanning
narrows at State Route 16,
Tacoma, Washington, vertical
and torsional motion viewed
from East Tower, November 7,
1940. Still from a 16 mm film
by Professor F. B. Farquharson,
University Of Washington.
From Library of Congress.

Brise-soleil, El Modulón,
Community Center, Mexico City,
Luis Vicente Flores, 1998.

Barcelona, the Rambla, cigarette card. From George Arents Collection, New York Public Library.

The second, widely televised demolition of a Pruitt-Igoe building, April 1972.

The Sphinx of Giza, partially excavated, with two pyramids in the background, 1878 (detail). From Library of Congress.

Suburbs photo, source unknown. From New York Public Library Picture Collection.

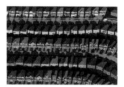

An aerial view of housing developments near Markham, Ontario, November 2005, photograph by Ian Duke.

A large block of ice being held by a man, 1942, photograph by Nina Leen. Life Picture Collection / Getty Images.

Torpedo bike, France, 1913. From Gallica / Bibliothèque nationale de France.

Wheels of yarn, photograph by H. E. Olson (detail). *MIT Technology Review*, June 1938, cover.

12-way, drawing by Steven Alps (detail). www.alpsroads.net.

Canceled stamps,
Germany, 1972.

*17 Feet Diameter Fir Tree
near McMurray, Wash.*, 1908,
photograph by Darius Kinsey.
Courtesy of the Getty's
Open Content Program.

Surgical scissors, source
unknown. From New York Public
Library Picture Collection.

Map of the Greenwich Village
section of New York City
(detail). New York Public Library
Digital Collections.

An elephant places his foot
on animal trainer Karl Fischer's
face at Maidstone Zoo, 1938,
photograph by Reg Speller
(detail). From Fox Photos /
Getty Images.

A stave irrigation pipe in position.
George Shuman and Co.,
*Our Wonder World: A Library
of Knowledge in Ten Volumes*,
vol. 4 (Chicago and Boston:
George L. Shuman, 1923), 362.

General plan of Versailles,
1700, Nicolas de Fer.
From Gallica / Bibliothèque
nationale de France.

Africa relief map,
Alex Everett Frye (detail).
Frye's Primary Geography
(Boston: Ginn, 1894), 362.

"Like Rays of Benediction
Bathing Some Cathedral
Throng," clipping, photograph
by Ewing Galloway. From Irma
and Paul Milstein Division
of United States History,
Local History and Genealogy,
New York Public Library.

Diamond (detail).
Victor Goldschmidt,
Atlas der Krystallformen,
vol. 3 (Heidelberg,
Germany: Carl Winter's
Universitätsbuchhandlung,
1913), 33.

Five-cent postcard, "Tonkin—
Baie d'Along, Parages des
Merveilles," sampan, Indochina,
1913.

Elevated railway curve at 110th
Street, New York, 1919.
From Picture Collection, Miriam
and Ira D. Wallach Division
of Art, Prints and Photographs,
Digital Collections, New York
Public Library.

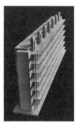

Model of an apartment building
for small apartments, Dessau,
Germany, 1924, Walter Gropius,
ed., *International Architecture*,
Bauhausbucher 1. (Munich:
Long, 1925), 90. Courtesy
of Heidelberg University.

Louis Armstrong, 1957,
photograph by a *New York
World-Telegram* staff
photographer (detail).
From Library of Congress.

Windy city, photographer
unknown. From New York Public
Library Picture Collection.

Houseplants,
source unknown.

Sun breaking through clouds,
Egyptian tarot, 1875–1899.
From Gallica / Bibliothèque
nationale de France.

Eye exam. A. Maitland Ramsay,
Eye Injuries and Their Treatment
(New York: Macmillan, 1907).

Boston Symphony Hall (detail). Charles Follen McKim, Richard Guy Wilson, Stanford White, and William Rutherford Mead, *The Architecture of McKim, Mead & White: Selected Works 1879–1915* (New York: Princeton Architectural Press, 2018), plate 141.

The intersection of Broadway, Fifth Avenue, and 23rd Street, as viewed from the top of the Flatiron Building, looking north. From Irma and Paul Milstein Division of United States History, Local History and Genealogy, New York Public Library.

Straw-bale secondary school, Malawi (detail). Courtesy of Nudes Architecture / Nuru Karim.

Biodiversity (detail). From New York Public Library Picture Collection.

Arizona cactus. © Kozo Miyoshi, courtesy of PGI.

A sectional view of the New York Public Library (detail). From Picture Collection, Miriam and Ira D. Wallach Division of Art, Prints and Photographs, Digital Collections, New York Public Library.

A sketch of a fresh apricot. Martin Frobenius Ledermüller, *Amusement Microscopique* (Nuremberg, Germany: Winterschmidt, 1768) Plate XXX. Courtesy of the Biodiversity Heritage Library.

Men doing exercises in a gymnastics wheel (*Rhönrad*), 1929. From Getty Images.

Paper nautilus. *South Australian Naturalist*, November 30, 1940, cover art.

Published by
Princeton Architectural Press
70 West 36th Street
New York, New York 10018
www.papress.com

Reprinted with permission from Michael Sorkin,
What Goes Up, London: Verso, 2018.

ISBN 978-1-64896-080-2
Library of Congress Control Number: 2021936582

Editor: Sara McKay
Designer: Benjamin English

Editor's note: This book was conceived in the fall
of 2019 in collaboration with Michael Sorkin.
It was completed in early 2021 with the guidance
of his wife, Joan Copjec.

Other books by Michael Sorkin

Exquisite Corpse: Writings on Buildings
Some Assembly Required
Starting from Zero: Reconstructing Downtown New York
Twenty Minutes in Manhattan
All Over the Map: Writing on Buildings and Cities
What Goes Up: The Right and Wrongs to the City